The Little Seed
A Parable
(Psalm 1: 1-3)

Randy Hartwell
Illustrations by Sydney Durrett

Write Way Publishing Company

The Little Seed

Copyright © 2018 by Randy Hartwell

All rights reserved. No part of this publication may be reproduced, distributed, or transmitted in any form or by any means, including photocopying, recording, or other electronic or mechanical methods, without the prior written permission of the publisher, except in the case of brief quotations embodied in critical reviews and certain other noncommercial uses permitted by copyright law. Permission requests should be sent to info@writewaypublishingcompany.com.

Printed in the United States of America
ISBN 978-1-946425-24-9

Book Design by CSinclaire Write-Design
Illustrations by Sydney Durrett
Cover Design by Sydney Durrett and Charlotte Sinclaire

Write Way Publishing Company LLC
Raleigh, NC

There was once a mighty tree that stood in a great forest. The tree gave cool shade to travelers, and many animals lived in its limbs and leaves.

The tree also dropped
small seeds,
which sometimes grew into
strong, beautiful trees.

One day a little seed
fell to the ground
with several others.
The tiny seed wanted
to grow into a great tree
just like her father.

She watched as seeds around
her began to sprout into saplings
and wondered when she, too,
would begin to grow.
But it was not to be.

It so happened that a desert was moving toward the forest. Day by day, the small trees that had grown up around the little seed were swallowed up in the hot sand and wilted.

And finally, she also was covered by the shifting desert sand.

For a while, the little seed wondered what had become of her brothers and sisters. She especially wondered what had happened to her father. They no longer seemed near her, and she was frightened by the silence and loneliness. But all she could do was wait in the quiet darkness under the sand.

The little seed began to feel that
her family had left her—
and she was angry! Why had
they not stayed with her?
She had tried so hard to be
good. And she had waited so
long to become a great tree.

As time passed, the little seed began to wonder if her father still loved her. Why would he leave her here alone if he did? Had he forgotten about her? And she was buried so deep, would he even be able to find her? Did he care enough to want to find her? Where had he gone?

In a while, the little seed
began to feel differently.
The sand was warm, and she
had not wilted in it, as had many
of her brothers and sisters.
She began to be glad that she
had not sprouted so quickly.
She would have surely withered
like some of her brothers and
sisters if she had.

After a time,
the desert moved on,
and the little seed
found herself no longer
covered by the sand.
But her brothers and sisters
were gone, and she could no
longer see her father.
Deep inside of her, though,
she had come to believe
that he was still with her.

One day not long after the sand had moved on, rain fell from a dark gray sky, one of the first seen in a very long time.
The dusty coating left on the little seed was washed away as she soaked up the water.

The next morning
the warm sun shone on her,
and she began to grow.
Day after day she grew
taller and stronger.

As time passed, the little seed grew into a mighty tree very much like her father. Travelers found coolness in her shade, and many animals lived in her branches. Her roots were planted deep in the rich earth. And when a hard wind blew, she swayed but would not be broken.

The great tree came to understand that she had not found her own way out of the desert and that she had been taken out at just the right time. She had become like her father by waiting for his strength to grow within her.

And she dropped
many good seeds
all her life.

ABOUT THE AUTHOR

Randy Hartwell lives in Durham, North Carolina, with his wife, Catherine, and is employed as a project manager in the biopharmaceutical industry. He enjoys reading, watching college football, and doing jobs around the house. In addition to co-authoring several technical articles (mostly concerning Mad Cow Disease), he has been creating stories for many years. *The Little Seed: A Parable* is his first published work of fiction.

ABOUT THE ILLUSTRATOR

Based in Charlotte, North Carolina, Sydney Durrett has organically grown Durrett Designs from a fun passion into a full-time profession. Her colorful portfolio and custom pieces for businesses and individuals feature cityscapes, skylines, animals and pet portraits, house portraits, landscapes, universities, and landmarks. *The Little Seed: A Parable* is her first book illustration project. You can see her work at www.durrettdesigns.com.

www.ingramcontent.com/pod-product-compliance
Lightning Source LLC
Chambersburg PA
CBHW042130040426
42450CB00003B/141